I0426164

# Bird Community Monitoring at Hopewell Culture National Historical Park, Ohio

*Status Report*

Natural Resource Data Series NPS/HTLN/NRDS—2012/232

David G. Peitz

National Park Service
The Heartland I&M Network
Wilson's Creek National Battlefield
6424 West Farm Road 182,
Republic, MO 65738

January 2012

U.S. Department of the Interior
National Park Service
Natural Resource Stewardship and Science
Fort Collins, Colorado

The National Park Service, Natural Resource Stewardship and Science office in Fort Collins, Colorado publishes a range of reports that address natural resource topics of interest and applicability to a broad audience in the National Park Service and others in natural resource management, including scientists, conservation and environmental constituencies, and the public.

The Natural Resource Data Series is intended for the timely release of basic data sets and data summaries. Care has been taken to assure accuracy of raw data values, but a thorough analysis and interpretation of the data has not been completed. Consequently, the initial analyses of data in this report are provisional and subject to change.

All manuscripts in the series receive the appropriate level of peer review to ensure that the information is scientifically credible, technically accurate, appropriately written for the intended audience, and designed and published in a professional manner. Data in this report were collected and analyzed using methods based on established, peer-reviewed protocols and were analyzed and interpreted within the guidelines of the protocols.

Views, statements, findings, conclusions, recommendations, and data in this report do not necessarily reflect views and policies of the National Park Service, U.S. Department of the Interior. Mention of trade names or commercial products does not constitute endorsement or recommendation for use by the U.S. Government.

This report is available from Heartland Network I&M Program website (http://www.nature.nps.gov/im/units/htln/) and the Natural Resource Publications Management website (http://www.nature.nps.gov/publications/nrpm/).

Please cite this publication as:

Peitz, D. G. 2012. Bird community monitoring at Hopewell Culture National Historical Park, Ohio: Status report. Natural Resource Data Series NPS/HTLN/NRDS—2012/232. National Park Service, Fort Collins, Colorado.

NPS 353/112479, January 2012

# Contents

# Figures

# Tables

# Introduction

Birds are an important component of park ecosystems, as their high body temperature, rapid metabolism, and high ecological position in most food webs make them good indicators of the effects of local and regional changes in ecosystems. It has been suggested that management activities aimed at preserving habitat for bird populations, such as for neotropical migrants, can have the added benefit of preserving entire ecosystems and their attendant ecosystem services (Karr 1991, Maurer 1993). Moreover, birds have a tremendous following among the public and many parks provide information on the status and trends of birds through their interpretive programs.

We use trends in community composition and abundance of bird populations as long-term indicators of ecosystem integrity in the varied habitats of Hopewell Culture National Historical Park, Ohio (HOCU). Ecosystem integrity is defined as the system's capability to support and maintain a balanced, integrated, adaptive community of organisms having a species composition, diversity, and functional organization comparable to that of the natural habitat of the region (Karr and Dudley 1981). Research has demonstrated that birds serve as good indicators of changes in ecosystems (Cairns et al. 2004, Mallory et al. 2006, Wood et al. 2006).

Therefore, changes in the population size and community composition of birds on the park may reflect the effectiveness of management in restoring and maintaining the various vegetative communities at HOCU. Long-term trends in community composition and abundance of breeding bird populations provide one measure for assessing the ecological integrity and sustainability of these systems.

# Methods

### Site Selection for Bird Plots

Permanent monitoring locations or 'plots' were selected by overlaying a systematic grid of 400 x 400 meter cells (originating from a random start point) across all units of HOCU. The orientation of the grid was rotated 45 degrees to prevent monitoring sites from being influenced by man-made features (roads, fences, etc.) located along cardinal directions. We established 27 permanent plots on HOCU for monitoring bird population sizes and community composition (Fig. 1).

During bird surveys, monitoring plots were located using navigation waypoints in a GPS unit. In years when habitat was assessed (2005 – 2007, 2011), plots were temporarily marked with 36-inch pin flags to aid in re-locating the plots for habitat assessment, eliminating the need for permanent plot markers. We collected pin flags from each plot once the habitat work was completed.

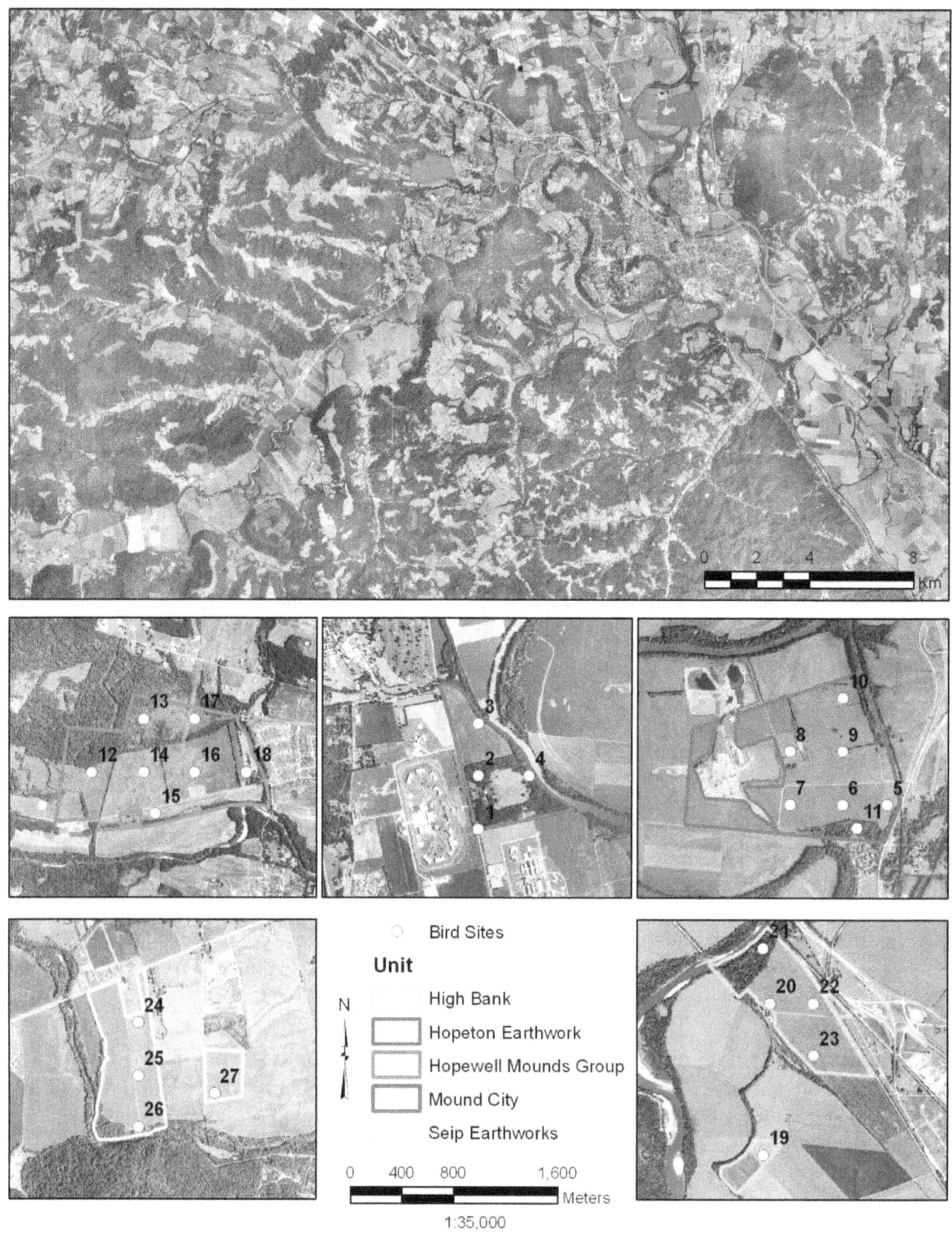

Figure 1. Bird plot locations on Hopewell Culture National Historical Park, Ohio.

2

## Bird Surveys

Bird surveys followed methods outlined in the bird monitoring protocol by Peitz et al. (2008) and summarized below. Variable circular plot counts, a point count methodology that incorporates a measure of detectability into population estimates, were used to survey birds present (Fancy 1997). All birds seen or heard at plots during 5-min sampling periods were counted along with their corresponding distance from observer. Bird observations were separated into two time segments: those detected during the first three minutes of the count (to allow future comparisons with the national Breeding Bird Survey data), and any new birds detected during the final two minutes of the count. For most species, we recorded each individual bird as a separate observation. For species that usually occur in clusters or flocks, the units recorded were cluster or flock size, and not the individual bird. During analysis, each individual in a cluster or flock were treated as a separate observations. After completing a count at a plot, and filling out the data sheet, the observer(s) navigated to the next plot using a GPS unit. While traveling between plots, the observer(s) was vigilant for the presence of species not recorded during timed surveys. These species help formulate a more complete species list for the park by identifying species missed during timed surveys. We sampled birds during a period when it was light enough to observe birds to four hours after sunrise. Table 1 list observers involved in monitoring birds, by year.

Table 1. Number of plots sampled, and sampling dates for breeding bird surveys conducted at Hopewell National Historical Park, Ohio, by year. Also listed are observer(s) who conducted the surveys and whether or not habitat data was collected during the survey year.

| Year | Sampling Dates | Number of Plots Sampled | Observer(s) | Habitat Data Collected |
|------|----------------|--------------------------|-------------|------------------------|
| 2005 | June 1 – June 3 | 27 | D.G. Peitz* | Yes |
| 2006 | May 31 – June 2 | 27 | D.G. Peitz* | Yes |
| 2007 | June 12 – June 13 | 27 | D.G. Peitz* | Yes |
| 2008 | May 9 – June 2 | 27 | D.L. Hess, C.L. Jones, J. Foor, D. Bostic, and W. Bostic | No |
| 2009 | May 23 – June 12 | 27 | D.L. Hess, D. Reiner, and C.L. Jones | No |
| 2010 | May 15 – June 7 | 27 | D.L. Hess, D. Reiner, and J.T. Nelson | No |
| 2011 | May 22 – May 24 | 26 | D.G. Peitz* | Yes |

*Heartland I&M Network staff.

## Bird Habitat

The collection of habitat data followed methods outlined in the bird monitoring protocol by Peitz et al. (2008). A summary of the sampling methods follows. Habitat data collection started after the first variable circular plot count was completed. Observers visited plots for habitat measures in the same order they were surveyed for birds to avoid disturbing birds on a plot prior to the survey. Once the habitat crew arrived at a plot, they set up the center subplot and completed all habitat measures for this subplot and the 50-m radius plot.

We characterized habitat available for each bird species on a number of different scales. The amounts of grassland, old field, or woodland vegetation types on each 50-m radius plot sampled were recorded. As plots were sampled, vertical vegetation structure was measured in 1-m increments up to 7.5 meters in height at four locations around the perimeter of the subplot using a graduated measuring rod. Locations were in the four cardinal directions. Vertical structure was recorded for deciduous and herbaceous vegetation. For plots in woodland habitat, trees were tallied by species and diameter at breast height (DBH) size class (<1.0 cm, 1.1 – 2.5 cm, 2.6 – 8.0 cm, 8.1 – 15.0 cm, 15.1 – 23.0 cm, 23.1 – 38.0 or >38.0 cm) on the subplot. Basal area, canopy cover, and tree height were measured on subplots as well, for those plots located in woodland habitat. Lastly, at all subplots, ground and foliar cover were recorded in a 1.78-m radius nested sample plot. Ground cover included deciduous and grass litter, bare soil, woody debris (>2.5 cm diameter), and unvegetated. Foliar cover was estimated for three plant guilds, including cool-season grasses, forbs, shrubs and vines, and total foliar cover (<1.5 m tall). Average parameter values were reported for grassland (open; including old field) and woodland plots separately.

## Data Analysis

Prior to summary analysis, the residency status (permanent resident, summer resident, migrant, and winter resident) of each bird species recorded was determined. Identifying the residency of each species helps to exclude migrants and winter residents from analysis of breeding birds within HOCU. Hereafter, permanent and summer resident birds are referred to as breeding species. The frequency and abundance of breeding bird species were determined two ways for both the grassland (open) and woodland habitats. First, for each breeding species, the number of individuals encountered per plot visit was determined (individuals / plot visit). And second, the proportion of plots occupied by each breeding species was determined (total number of plots occupied by a species / total number of plots visited).

Averages ($\pm$ std dev) for semi-permanent plot data, including grassland, old field, or woodland vegetation were calculated from plot estimates. Averages ($\pm$ std dev) for basal area, canopy cover, and tree height were calculated from plot estimates for woodland plots. Average ($\pm$ std dev) vertical structure diversity was estimated and reported for grassland (open) and woodland plots separately.

$$\text{Structural Diversity Index} = \frac{((\sum p_i / 8) + a) * 100}{2}$$

Where $p_i$ – is the observed frequency for vegetation in the $i$th interval touching a measuring rod out of eight measuring events, and $a$ – is the percent of intervals with recorded vegetation in eight height increments. Vertical structure diversity values are weighted equally to represent both the vertical height of vegetation and how dense the vegetation is within each height increment.

Within each habitat, ground cover, including deciduous or grass litter, bare soil, woody debris (>2.5 cm DBH; woodland plots), and unvegetated were averaged ($\pm$ std dev) across plots. Foliar cover, by guild of cool-season grasses, forbs, shrubs and vines (woodland plots), and total foliar cover (<1.5 m tall) were averaged ($\pm$ std dev) across plots as well. Also reported are species compositions of trees by family and size classes.

# Results

## Bird Surveys

Ninety-six bird species were recorded from 2005 and 2011during the breeding bird surveys at HOCU (Table 2). Eighty-nine of the 96 species recorded are classified as permanent or summer residents (Stokes and Stokes 1995). Therefore, these 89 species can be considered breeding species on the park. Classification of the remaining species is migrants with the exception of one winter resident, the Bald Eagle (*Haliaeetus leucocephalus*). Seven breeding species and one migrant, the Yellow-rumped Warbler (*Dendroica coronate*) were only observed outside 5-min survey periods. Twenty breeding species were observed exclusively in grassland (open) habitats (Tables 3 and 4). Also, within the grassland habitats (open), six breeding grassland obligate species were observed. Seven breeding species were observed exclusively in woodland habitats (Tables 5 and 6). Six species--American Robin (*Turdus migratorius*), Common Yellowthroat (*Geothlypis trichas*), Eastern Towhee (*Pipilo erythrophthalmus*), Field Sparrow (*Spizella pusilla*), Northern Cardinal (*Cardinalis cardinalis*), and Red-winged Blackbird (*Agelaius phoeniceus*)--were recorded in both grassland (open) and woodland habitats, in all years.

Fifteen breeding species--Acadian Flycatcher (*Empidonax virescens*), Blue-winged Warbler (*Vermivora pinus*) Brown Thrasher (*Toxostoma rufum*), Carolina Wren (*Thryothorus ludovicianus*), Dickcissel (*Spiza americana*), Eastern Towhee, Grasshopper Sparrow (*Ammodramus savannarum*), Henslow's Sparrow (*Ammodramus henslowii*), Indigo Bunting (*Passerina cyanea*), Red-bellied Woodpecker (*Melanerpes carolinus*), White-eyed Vireo (*Vireo griseus*), Willow Flycatcher (*Empidonax traillii*), Wood Thrush (*Hylocichla mustelina*), Yellow-throated Vireo (*Vireo flavifrons*), and Yellow-throated Warbler (*Dendroica dominica*)--are considered species of continental importance (Rich et al. 2004). The Bald Eagle, Prairie Warbler (*Dendroica discolor*), and Tennessee Warbler (*Vermivora peregrina*) are also species of continental importance.

The Red-winged Blackbird is the most common breeding species in grassland (open) habitats across all years, followed by the Eastern Meadowlark (*Sturnella magna*), Song Sparrow (*Melospiza melodia*), Field Sparrow, Tree Swallow (*Tachycineta bicolor*), Common Yellowthroat, Grasshopper Sparrow, and Indigo Bunting. The American Robin is the most common breeding species in woodland habitats across all years, followed by the Northern Cardinal, Red-winged Blackbird, and Common Yellowthroat. Five species—Bewick's Wren (*Thryomanes bewickii*), Cliff Swallow (*Petrochelidon pyrrhonota*), Green Heron (*Butorides virescens*), Sedge Wren (*Cistothorus platensis*), and Wood Duck (*Aix sponsa*) were represented by observations from a single survey year.

Table 2. Bird species recorded during breeding bird surveys at Hopewell Culture National Historical Park, Ohio in 2005 – 2011. Residency status of each species is given.

| Common name | Species name | AOU code | Residency[1] |
|---|---|---|---|
| **Acadian Flycatcher** | ***Empidonax virescens*** | **ACFL** | **SR** |
| American Coot | *Fulica americana* | AMCO | M |
| American Crow | *Corvus brachyrhynchos* | AMCR | R |
| American Goldfinch | *Carduelis tristis* | AMGO | R |
| American Redstart | *Setophaga ruticilla* | AMRE | SR |
| American Robin | *Turdus migratorius* | AMRO | R |
| American Woodcock* | *Scolopax minor* | AMWO | SR |
| **Bald Eagle** | ***Haliaeetus leucocephalus*** | **BAEA** | **WR** |
| Bank Swallow | *Riparia riparia* | BANS | SR |
| Barn Swallow | *Hirundo rustica* | BARS | SR |
| Belted Kingfisher | *Ceryle alcyon* | BEKI | R |
| Bewick's Wren | *Thryomanes bewickii* | BEWR | SR |
| Black-throated Blue Warbler* | *Dendroica caerulescens* | BTBW | SR |
| Blue Grosbeak | *Guiraca caerulea* | BLGR | SR |
| Blue Jay | *Cyanocitta cristata* | BLJA | R |
| Blackpoll Warbler | *Dendroica striata* | BLPW | M |
| Bobolink | *Dolichonyx oryzivorus* | BOBO | M |
| Blue-gray Gnatcatcher | *Polioptila caerulea* | BGGN | SR |
| **Blue-winged Warbler** | ***Vermivora pinus*** | **BWWA** | **SR** |
| **Brown Thrasher** | ***Toxostoma rufum*** | **BRTH** | **SR** |
| Brown-headed Cowbird | *Molothrus ater* | BHCO | R |
| Canada Goose | *Branta canadensis* | CAGO | R |
| Carolina Chickadee | *Parus carolinensis* | CACH | R |
| **Carolina Wren** | ***Thryothorus ludovicianus*** | **CARW** | **R** |
| Cedar Waxwing | *Bombycilla cedrorum* | CEDW | R |
| Chipping Sparrow | *Spizella passerina* | CHSP | SR |
| Chimney Swift | *Chaetura pelagica* | CHSW | SR |
| Cliff Swallow | *Petrochelidon pyrrhonota* | CLSW | SR |
| Common Grackle | *Quiscalus quiscula* | COGR | R |
| Cooper's Hawk | *Accipiter cooperii* | COHA | R |
| Common Yellowthroat | *Geothlypis trichas* | COYE | SR |
| **Dickcissel** | ***Spiza americana*** | **DICK** | **SR** |
| Downy Woodpecker | *Picoides pubescens* | DOWO | R |
| **Eastern (Rufous-side) Towhee** | ***Pipilo erythrophthalmus*** | **EATO** | **R** |
| Eastern Bluebird | *Sialia sialis* | EABL | R |
| Eastern Kingbird | *Tyrannus tyrannus* | EAKI | SR |
| Eastern Meadowlark | *Sturnella magna* | EAME | R |
| Eastern Phoebe | *Sayornis phoebe* | EAPH | SR |
| Eastern Wood-pewee | *Contopus virens* | EAWP | SR |
| European Starling | *Sturnus vulgaris* | EUST | R |
| Field Sparrow | *Spizella pusilla* | FISP | R |
| **Grasshopper Sparrow** | ***Ammodramus savannarum*** | **GRSP** | **SR** |
| Gray Catbird | *Dumetella carolinensis* | GRCA | SR |

Table 2. Bird species recorded during breeding bird surveys at Hopewell Culture National Historical Park, Ohio in 2005 – 2011. Residency status of each species is given (continued).

| Common name | Species name | AOU code | Residency[T] |
|---|---|---|---|
| Great Blue Heron | *Ardea herodias* | GBHE | SR |
| Great Crested Flycatcher | *Myiarchus crinitus* | GCFL | SR |
| Green Heron | *Butorides virescens* | GRHE | SR |
| **Henslow's Sparrow** | ***Ammodramus henslowii*** | **HESP** | **SR** |
| Horned Lark* | *Eremophila alpestris* | HOLA | R |
| House Finch | *Carpodacus mexicanus* | HOFI | R |
| House Sparrow | *Passer domesticus* | HOSP | R |
| House Wren | *Troglodytes aedon* | HOWR | SR |
| **Indigo Bunting** | ***Passerina cyanea*** | **INBU** | **SR** |
| Killdeer | *Charadrius vociferous* | KILL | R |
| Least Flycatcher | *Empidonax minimus* | LEFL | SR |
| Mallard | *Anas platyrhynchos* | MALL | R |
| Mourning Dove | *Zenaida macroura* | MODO | R |
| (Myrtle) Yellow-rumped Warbler* | *Dendroica coronata* | MYWA | M |
| Northern (Baltimore) Oriole | *Icterus galbula* | BAOR | SR |
| Northern (Yellow-shafted) Flicker | *Colaptes auratus* | YSFL | R |
| Northern Bobwhite | *Colinus virginianus* | NOBO | R |
| Northern Cardinal | *Cardinalis cardinalis* | NOCA | R |
| Northern Mockingbird | *Minus polyglottos* | NOMO | R |
| Northern Parula* | *Parula americana* | NOPA | SR |
| Northern Rough-winged Swallow | *Stelgidopteryx serripennis* | NRWS | SR |
| Orchard Oriole | *Icterus spurious* | OROR | SR |
| Pileated Woodpecker* | *Dryocopus pileatus* | PIWO | R |
| **Prairie Warbler** | ***Dendroica discolor*** | **PRAW** | **M** |
| Purple Martin | *Progne subis* | PUMA | SR |
| **Red-bellied Woodpecker** | ***Melanerpes carolinus*** | **RBWO** | **R** |
| Red-eyed Vireo | *Vireo olivaceus* | REVI | SR |
| Red-tailed Hawk | *Buteo jamaicensis* | RTHA | R |
| Red-winged Blackbird | *Agelaius phoeniceus* | RWBL | R |
| Rose-breasted Grosbeak* | *Pheucticus ludovicianus* | RBGR | SR |
| Ring-necked Pheasant | *Phasianus colchicus* | RPHE | R |
| Rock Dove | *Columba livia* | RODO | R |
| Ruby-throated Hummingbird | *Archilochus colubris* | RTHU | SR |
| Savannah Sparrow | *Passerculus sandwichensis* | SAVS | SR |
| Scarlet Tanager | *Piranga olivacea* | SCTA | SR |
| Sedge Wren | *Cistothorus platensis* | SEWR | SR |
| Song Sparrow | *Melospiza melodia* | SOSP | R |
| Summer Tanager* | *Piranga rubra* | SUTA | SR |
| **Tennessee Warbler** | ***Vermivora peregrina*** | **TEWA** | **M** |
| Tree Swallow | *Tachycineta bicolor* | TRES | SR |
| (Eastern) Tufted titmouse | *Baeolophus bicolor* | ETTI | R |
| Turkey Vulture | *Cathartes aura* | TUVU | SR |
| Warbling Vireo | *Vireo gilvus* | WAVI | SR |

Table 2. Bird species recorded during breeding bird surveys at Hopewell Culture National Historical Park, Ohio in 2005 – 2011. Residency status of each species is given (continued).

| Common name | Species name | AOU code | Residency[1] |
|---|---|---|---|
| White-breasted Nuthatch | *Sitta carolinensis* | WBNU | R |
| **White-eyed Vireo** | ***Vireo griseus*** | **WEVI** | **SR** |
| **Willow Flycatcher** | ***Empidonax traillii*** | **WIFL** | **SR** |
| Wood Duck | *Aix sponsa* | WODU | SR |
| **Wood Thrush** | ***Hylocichla mustelina*** | **WOTH** | **SR** |
| Yellow Warbler | *Dendroica petechia* | YWAR | SR |
| Yellow-billed Cuckoo | *Coccyzus americanus* | YBCU | SR |
| Yellow-breasted Chat | *Icteria virens* | YBCH | SR |
| **Yellow-throated Vireo** | ***Vireo flavifrons*** | **YTVI** | **SR** |
| **Yellow-throated Warbler** | ***Dendroica dominica*** | **YTWA** | **SR** |

[*] Species recorded while traveling between point transects or at other times outside of 5-min survey periods.

[1] Residency: M = migrant; SR = summer resident; R = year around resident; WR = winter resident; According to Stokes and Stokes (1995).

Species names are valid and verified names taken from ITIS (Integrated Taxonomic Information System). http://www.itis.usda.gov/.

Bolded species names are those species considered of continental importance (Rich et al. 2004).

Table 3. Number of individuals encountered per plot visit (including flyovers) in grassland (open) habitats, averaged over plots sampled (n), for bird species recorded at Hopewell Culture National Historical Park, Ohio during breeding bird surveys. Individual species results are listed by year, 2005-2011.

| Common name | 2005 (n=20) | 2006 (n=20) | 2007 (n=20) | 2008 (n=20) | 2009 (n=20) | 2010 (n=20) | 2011 (n=20) |
|---|---|---|---|---|---|---|---|
| **Acadian Flycatcher** | -- | -- | -- | -- | 0.05 | -- | -- |
| American Crow | 0.10 | 0.15 | 0.05 | 0.15 | 0.50 | 0.05 | 0.05 |
| American Goldfinch | 0.15 | 0.45 | 0.35 | 0.45 | 0.45 | 1.10 | -- |
| American Robin | 0.15 | 0.05 | 0.10 | 0.20 | 0.25 | 0.80 | 0.05 |
| Bank Swallow* | -- | 0.05 | -- | -- | 0.15 | 0.65 | -- |
| Barn Swallow* | -- | 0.05 | -- | 0.30 | 0.15 | 0.35 | 0.10 |
| Bewick's Wren | -- | 0.05 | -- | -- | -- | -- | -- |
| Blue Grosbeak* | -- | 0.25 | 0.05 | -- | 0.05 | 0.05 | -- |
| Blue Jay | 0.05 | 0.10 | 0.05 | 0.25 | 0.20 | 0.25 | -- |
| Blue-gray Gnatcatcher | -- | -- | -- | 0.05 | 0.15 | -- | -- |
| **Blue-winged Warbler** | -- | -- | -- | 0.05 | -- | -- | -- |
| **Brown Thrasher** | -- | **0.20** | **0.15** | **0.20** | **0.10** | **0.20** | **0.10** |
| Brown-headed Cowbird | 0.05 | 0.10 | -- | -- | 0.10 | 0.05 | 0.05 |
| Canada Goose | -- | -- | -- | 0.30 | -- | 0.80 | -- |
| Carolina Chickadee | -- | -- | -- | -- | -- | 0.05 | -- |
| **Carolina Wren** | **0.15** | **0.15** | **0.05** | **0.10** | **0.05** | **0.05** | -- |
| Cedar Waxwing | -- | -- | -- | -- | -- | 0.45 | -- |
| Chimney Swift | -- | -- | -- | 0.10 | 0.50 | 0.20 | 0.20 |
| Cliff Swallow* | -- | -- | -- | -- | -- | 0.05 | -- |
| Common Grackle | -- | -- | 0.20 | 0.85 | 2.55 | 2.10 | -- |
| Cooper's Hawk | -- | -- | -- | 0.05 | -- | -- | -- |
| Common Yellowthroat | 0.25 | 0.05 | 0.45 | 0.70 | 0.55 | 0.55 | 0.45 |
| **Dickcissel*,[1]** | **0.90** | **0.25** | **0.35** | **0.15** | **0.50** | **0.10** | -- |
| Downy Woodpecker | -- | -- | 0.05 | -- | -- | 0.05 | -- |
| **Eastern (Rufous-side) Towhee** | **0.10** | **0.05** | **0.15** | **0.35** | **0.10** | **0.25** | **0.05** |
| Eastern Bluebird | -- | 0.20 | -- | 0.10 | 0.10 | -- | -- |
| Eastern Kingbird | -- | 0.05 | -- | 0.25 | 0.10 | 0.15 | -- |
| Eastern Meadowlark[1] | 0.45 | 0.35 | 0.20 | 0.85 | 1.35 | 1.80 | 0.25 |
| Eastern Phoebe* | 0.05 | -- | -- | -- | -- | 0.05 | -- |
| Eastern Wood-pewee | -- | 0.05 | -- | 0.10 | 0.10 | 0.10 | -- |
| European Starling | 0.05 | -- | 0.25 | 0.50 | 0.90 | 1.60 | 0.25 |
| Field Sparrow | 0.30 | 0.45 | 0.70 | 0.70 | 0.60 | 0.60 | 0.25 |
| **Grasshopper Sparrow*,[1]** | **0.60** | **0.50** | **0.20** | **0.25** | **0.40** | **0.45** | **0.35** |
| Gray Catbird | -- | -- | 0.05 | 0.15 | 0.15 | 0.25 | -- |
| Great Blue Heron* | 0.10 | 0.15 | -- | 0.15 | 0.25 | 0.15 | 0.15 |
| Great Crested Flycatcher | -- | -- | -- | -- | -- | -- | 0.05 |
| Green Heron* | -- | -- | -- | -- | -- | -- | 0.10 |
| **Henslow's Sparrow*,[1]** | **0.10** | **0.10** | **0.15** | -- | **0.25** | **0.45** | -- |
| House Finch* | 0.05 | -- | -- | -- | 0.05 | 0.15 | -- |
| House Wren | -- | -- | 0.10 | 0.25 | 0.20 | 0.30 | 0.05 |
| **Indigo Bunting** | **0.35** | **0.25** | **0.50** | **0.25** | **0.40** | **0.60** | **0.35** |

9

Table 3. Number of individuals encountered per plot visit (including flyovers) in grassland (open) habitats, averaged over plots sampled (n), for bird species recorded at Hopewell Culture National Historical Park, Ohio during breeding bird surveys. Individual species results are listed by year, 2005-2011 (continued).

| Common name | 2005 (n=20) | 2006 (n=20) | 2007 (n=20) | 2008 (n=20) | 2009 (n=20) | 2010 (n=20) | 2011 (n=20) |
|---|---|---|---|---|---|---|---|
| Killdeer* | -- | -- | -- | -- | 0.10 | 0.10 | -- |
| Mallard* | -- | -- | -- | -- | 0.05 | -- | 0.10 |
| Mourning Dove | 0.05 | 0.15 | 0.15 | 0.80 | 0.50 | 0.60 | -- |
| Northern (Baltimore) Oriole | 0.05 | -- | 0.05 | 0.10 | 0.10 | 0.25 | -- |
| Northern (Yellow-shafted) Flicker | -- | -- | -- | -- | 0.20 | 0.10 | -- |
| Northern Bobwhite* | 0.20 | 0.10 | 0.05 | -- | -- | -- | -- |
| Northern Cardinal | 0.20 | 0.10 | 0.40 | 0.25 | 0.50 | 0.25 | 0.10 |
| Northern Mockingbird | -- | -- | 0.10 | -- | 0.10 | -- | 0.05 |
| Northern Rough-winged Swallow* | -- | -- | 0.05 | 0.25 | 0.40 | 0.35 | -- |
| Orchard Oriole | -- | -- | 0.10 | 0.25 | 0.15 | 0.20 | -- |
| Purple Martin | -- | -- | -- | -- | -- | 0.05 | -- |
| **Red-bellied Woodpecker** | -- | -- | -- | 0.10 | 0.15 | 0.10 | -- |
| Red-eyed Vireo | 0.05 | 0.05 | -- | 0.05 | 0.35 | 0.15 | -- |
| Red-tailed Hawk* | 0.05 | 0.05 | 0.10 | 0.05 | -- | 0.20 | -- |
| Red-winged Blackbird | 4.50 | 3.60 | 3.85 | 3.60 | 4.65 | 2.90 | 3.05 |
| Ring-necked Pheasant | 0.30 | 0.05 | 0.05 | 0.05 | 0.20 | 0.05 | -- |
| Rock Dove | 0.10 | -- | -- | -- | 0.15 | -- | -- |
| Ruby-throated Hummingbird | -- | -- | -- | -- | 0.05 | 0.05 | -- |
| Savannah Sparrow*[1] | -- | -- | -- | 0.05 | -- | -- | 0.05 |
| Scarlet Tanager | -- | -- | -- | 0.05 | 0.05 | -- | -- |
| Sedge Wren*[1] | -- | -- | 0.05 | -- | -- | -- | -- |
| Song Sparrow | 0.40 | 0.20 | 0.45 | 0.90 | 0.80 | 0.90 | 0.25 |
| Tree Swallow | 0.80 | 0.05 | 0.45 | 0.55 | 0.35 | 0.30 | 0.60 |
| (Eastern) Tufted Titmouse | 0.10 | 0.10 | -- | 0.30 | 0.20 | 0.20 | -- |
| Turkey Vulture* | 0.05 | -- | -- | 0.20 | 0.75 | -- | -- |
| Warbling Vireo | -- | -- | 0.05 | -- | 0.10 | 0.10 | -- |
| **White-eyed Vireo** | -- | -- | 0.05 | 0.35 | 0.15 | 0.10 | -- |
| **Willow Flycatcher** | -- | -- | 0.10 | 0.05 | 0.45 | 0.30 | -- |
| Wood Duck* | -- | -- | 0.05 | -- | -- | -- | -- |
| **Wood Thrush** | -- | -- | 0.05 | 0.20 | 0.15 | 0.10 | -- |
| Yellow Warbler | 0.10 | 0.20 | 0.05 | 0.25 | 0.35 | 0.25 | -- |
| Yellow-billed Cuckoo | -- | -- | 0.05 | 0.05 | 0.10 | -- | -- |
| Yellow-breasted Chat | 0.15 | 0.30 | 0.10 | 0.30 | 0.25 | 0.30 | 0.15 |
| **Yellow-throated Vireo** | -- | -- | 0.05 | -- | -- | -- | -- |

* Species recorded exclusively in grassland (open) habitats.

[1] Grassland obligate.

Bolded species names are those species considered of continental importance (Rich et al. 2004).

Table 4. Proportion of plots (n) occupied annually by bird species (including flyovers) in grassland (open) habitats at Hopewell Culture National Historical Park, Ohio during breeding bird surveys. Individual species results are listed by year, 2005-2011.

| Common name | 2005 (n=20) | 2006 (n=20) | 2007 (n=20) | 2008 (n=20) | 2009 (n=20) | 2010 (n=20) | 2011 (n=20) |
|---|---|---|---|---|---|---|---|
| **Acadian Flycatcher** | -- | -- | -- | -- | 0.05 | -- | -- |
| American Crow | 0.10 | 0.10 | 0.05 | 0.15 | 0.30 | 0.05 | 0.05 |
| American Goldfinch | 0.05 | 0.15 | 0.20 | 0.20 | 0.20 | 0.55 | -- |
| American Robin | 0.15 | 0.05 | 0.10 | 0.20 | 0.20 | 0.55 | 0.05 |
| Bank Swallow* | -- | 0.05 | -- | -- | 0.05 | 0.20 | -- |
| Barn Swallow* | -- | 0.05 | -- | 0.30 | 0.10 | 0.30 | 0.10 |
| Bewick's Wren | -- | 0.05 | -- | -- | -- | -- | -- |
| Blue Grosbeak* | -- | 0.05 | 0.05 | -- | 0.05 | 0.05 | -- |
| Blue Jay | 0.05 | 0.10 | 0.05 | 0.20 | 0.15 | 0.25 | -- |
| Blue-gray Gnatcatcher | -- | -- | -- | 0.05 | 0.15 | -- | -- |
| **Blue-winged Warbler** | -- | -- | -- | 0.05 | -- | -- | -- |
| **Brown Thrasher** | -- | 0.15 | 0.15 | 0.20 | 0.10 | 0.20 | 0.10 |
| Brown-headed Cowbird | 0.05 | 0.05 | -- | -- | 0.10 | 0.05 | 0.05 |
| Canada Goose | -- | -- | -- | 0.05 | -- | 0.10 | -- |
| Carolina Chickadee | -- | -- | -- | -- | -- | 0.05 | -- |
| **Carolina Wren** | 0.15 | 0.15 | 0.05 | 0.10 | 0.05 | 0.05 | -- |
| Cedar Waxwing | -- | -- | -- | -- | -- | 0.20 | -- |
| Chimney Swift | -- | -- | -- | 0.05 | 0.25 | 0.10 | 0.05 |
| Cliff Swallow* | -- | -- | -- | -- | -- | 0.05 | -- |
| Common Grackle | -- | -- | 0.10 | 0.60 | 0.55 | 0.90 | -- |
| Cooper's Hawk | -- | -- | -- | 0.05 | -- | -- | -- |
| Common Yellowthroat | 0.15 | 0.05 | 0.35 | 0.65 | 0.55 | 0.50 | 0.45 |
| **Dickcissel*[1]** | 0.30 | 0.15 | 0.25 | 0.10 | 0.20 | 0.10 | -- |
| Downy Woodpecker | -- | -- | 0.05 | -- | -- | 0.05 | -- |
| **Eastern (Rufous-side) Towhee** | 0.10 | 0.05 | 0.15 | 0.35 | 0.10 | 0.25 | 0.05 |
| Eastern Bluebird | -- | 0.10 | -- | 0.10 | 0.10 | -- | -- |
| Eastern Kingbird | -- | 0.05 | -- | 0.25 | 0.05 | 0.10 | -- |
| Eastern Meadowlark[1] | 0.45 | 0.25 | 0.15 | 0.55 | 0.75 | 0.70 | 0.20 |
| Eastern Phoebe* | 0.05 | -- | -- | -- | -- | 0.05 | -- |
| Eastern Wood-pewee | -- | 0.05 | -- | 0.10 | 0.10 | 0.10 | -- |
| European Starling | 0.05 | -- | 0.20 | 0.35 | 0.40 | 0.45 | 0.05 |
| Field Sparrow | 0.30 | 0.25 | 0.40 | 0.70 | 0.45 | 0.45 | 0.20 |
| **Grasshopper Sparrow*[1]** | 0.25 | 0.35 | 0.20 | 0.25 | 0.25 | 0.40 | 0.25 |
| Gray Catbird | -- | -- | 0.05 | 0.15 | 0.15 | 0.25 | -- |
| Great Blue Heron* | 0.10 | 0.10 | -- | 0.10 | 0.15 | 0.15 | 0.05 |
| Great Crested Flycatcher | -- | -- | -- | -- | -- | -- | 0.05 |
| Green Heron* | -- | -- | -- | -- | -- | -- | 0.05 |
| **Henslow's Sparrow*[1]** | 0.05 | 0.05 | 0.05 | -- | 0.10 | 0.25 | -- |
| House Finch* | 0.05 | -- | -- | -- | 0.05 | 0.05 | -- |
| House Wren | -- | -- | 0.10 | 0.25 | 0.15 | 0.25 | 0.05 |
| **Indigo Bunting** | 0.20 | 0.20 | 0.35 | 0.25 | 0.30 | 0.45 | 0.25 |

Table 4. Proportion of plots (n) occupied annually by bird species (including flyovers) in grassland (open) habitats at Hopewell Culture National Historical Park, Ohio during breeding bird surveys. Individual species results are listed by year, 2005-2011 (continued).

| Common name | 2005 (n=20) | 2006 (n=20) | 2007 (n=20) | 2008 (n=20) | 2009 (n=20) | 2010 (n=20) | 2011 (n=20) |
|---|---|---|---|---|---|---|---|
| Killdeer* | -- | -- | -- | -- | 0.10 | 0.10 | -- |
| Mallard* | -- | -- | -- | -- | 0.05 | -- | 0.05 |
| Mourning Dove | 0.05 | 0.05 | 0.10 | 0.45 | 0.30 | 0.35 | -- |
| Northern (Baltimore) Oriole | 0.05 | -- | 0.05 | 0.05 | 0.10 | 0.25 | -- |
| Northern (Yellow-shafted) Flicker | -- | -- | -- | -- | 0.20 | 0.10 | -- |
| Northern Bobwhite* | 0.15 | 0.05 | 0.05 | -- | -- | -- | -- |
| Northern Cardinal | 0.20 | 0.10 | 0.30 | 0.25 | 0.45 | 0.20 | 0.10 |
| Northern Mockingbird | -- | -- | 0.10 | -- | 0.10 | -- | 0.05 |
| Northern Rough-winged Swallow* | -- | -- | 0.05 | 0.10 | 0.25 | 0.20 | -- |
| Orchard Oriole | -- | -- | 0.10 | 0.25 | 0.15 | 0.15 | -- |
| Purple Martin | -- | -- | -- | -- | -- | 0.05 | -- |
| **Red-bellied Woodpecker** | -- | -- | -- | **0.10** | **0.15** | **0.10** | -- |
| Red-eyed Vireo | 0.05 | 0.05 | -- | 0.05 | 0.35 | 0.15 | -- |
| Red-tailed Hawk* | 0.05 | 0.05 | 0.10 | 0.05 | -- | 0.15 | -- |
| Red-winged Blackbird | 0.80 | 0.80 | 0.85 | 0.95 | 0.90 | 0.90 | 0.95 |
| Ring-necked Pheasant | 0.30 | 0.05 | 0.05 | 0.05 | 0.10 | 0.05 | -- |
| Rock Dove | 0.05 | -- | -- | -- | 0.10 | -- | -- |
| Ruby-throated Hummingbird | -- | -- | -- | -- | 0.05 | 0.05 | -- |
| Savannah Sparrow*,[1] | -- | -- | -- | 0.05 | -- | -- | 0.05 |
| Scarlet Tanager | -- | -- | -- | 0.05 | 0.05 | -- | -- |
| Sedge Wren*,[1] | -- | -- | 0.05 | -- | -- | -- | -- |
| Song Sparrow | 0.30 | 0.05 | 0.35 | 0.75 | 0.55 | 0.65 | 0.15 |
| Tree Swallow | 0.30 | 0.05 | 0.10 | 0.30 | 0.20 | 0.20 | 0.25 |
| (Eastern) Tufted Titmouse | 0.05 | 0.05 | -- | 0.30 | 0.15 | 0.15 | -- |
| Turkey Vulture* | 0.05 | -- | -- | 0.15 | 0.10 | -- | -- |
| Warbling Vireo | -- | -- | 0.05 | -- | 0.10 | 0.10 | -- |
| **White-eyed Vireo** | -- | -- | **0.05** | **0.35** | **0.15** | **0.10** | -- |
| **Willow Flycatcher** | -- | -- | **0.10** | **0.05** | **0.40** | **0.30** | -- |
| Wood Duck* | -- | -- | 0.05 | -- | -- | -- | -- |
| **Wood Thrush** | -- | -- | **0.05** | **0.20** | **0.15** | **0.10** | -- |
| Yellow Warbler | 0.10 | 0.15 | 0.05 | 0.25 | 0.35 | 0.25 | -- |
| Yellow-billed Cuckoo | -- | -- | 0.05 | 0.05 | 0.10 | -- | -- |
| Yellow-breasted Chat | 0.15 | 0.25 | 0.10 | 0.30 | 0.15 | 0.25 | 0.15 |
| **Yellow-throated Vireo** | -- | -- | **0.05** | -- | -- | -- | -- |

* Species recorded exclusively in grassland (open) habitats.

[1] Grassland obligate.

Bolded species names are those species considered of continental importance (Rich et al. 2004).

Table 5. Number of individuals encountered per plot visit (including flyovers) in woodlands, averaged over plots sampled (n), for bird species recorded at Hopewell Culture National Historical Park, Ohio during breeding bird surveys. Individual species results are listed by year, 2005-2011.

| Common name | 2005 (n=7) | 2006 (n=7) | 2007 (n=7) | 2008 (n=7) | 2009 (n=7) | 2010 (n=7) | 2011 (n=6) |
|---|---|---|---|---|---|---|---|
| **Acadian Flycatcher** | -- | -- | 0.14 | -- | -- | 0.14 | -- |
| American Crow | -- | -- | -- | -- | 0.29 | 0.14 | -- |
| American Goldfinch | -- | -- | -- | 0.14 | 0.14 | 0.43 | -- |
| American Redstart* | -- | -- | -- | 0.14 | -- | 0.14 | -- |
| American Robin | 0.71 | 0.86 | 0.86 | 0.14 | 1.43 | 1.00 | 0.50 |
| Belted Kingfisher* | 0.14 | 0.14 | -- | -- | -- | -- | -- |
| Bewick's Wren | -- | 0.57 | -- | -- | -- | -- | -- |
| Blue Jay | -- | -- | 0.14 | 0.43 | 0.14 | 0.43 | 0.33 |
| Blue-gray Gnatcatcher | 0.14 | -- | 0.14 | 0.43 | -- | 0.57 | -- |
| **Blue-winged Warbler** | -- | 0.14 | -- | -- | -- | -- | -- |
| **Brown Thrasher** | -- | -- | -- | 0.14 | 0.14 | -- | 0.17 |
| Brown-headed Cowbird | -- | -- | -- | 0.29 | 0.43 | 0.57 | -- |
| Canada Goose | -- | 1.43 | -- | 0.14 | 0.14 | 0.29 | -- |
| Carolina Chickadee | -- | -- | 0.29 | -- | -- | 0.14 | -- |
| **Carolina Wren** | **0.86** | -- | **0.29** | **0.29** | **0.43** | **0.43** | -- |
| Cedar Waxwing | -- | -- | -- | 0.29 | 0.14 | -- | -- |
| Chipping Sparrow* | -- | -- | -- | -- | 0.14 | 0.14 | 0.17 |
| Chimney Swift | -- | -- | -- | -- | 0.29 | 0.14 | -- |
| Common Grackle | -- | -- | -- | 0.14 | 1.43 | 0.71 | -- |
| Cooper's Hawk | -- | -- | -- | -- | -- | -- | 0.17 |
| Common Yellowthroat | 0.14 | 0.29 | 0.14 | 0.57 | 0.43 | 0.71 | 0.17 |
| Downy Woodpecker | -- | -- | -- | 0.14 | 0.43 | 0.43 | -- |
| **Eastern (Rufous-side) Towhee** | **0.14** | **0.14** | **0.29** | **0.43** | **0.29** | **0.43** | **0.17** |
| Eastern Bluebird | -- | -- | -- | 0.29 | -- | -- | -- |
| Eastern Kingbird | -- | -- | -- | -- | 0.14 | -- | -- |
| Eastern Meadowlark | -- | -- | -- | 0.14 | -- | 0.14 | -- |
| Eastern Wood-pewee | 0.14 | 0.57 | 0.29 | 0.29 | 0.14 | 0.14 | -- |
| European Starling | -- | 0.14 | 0.57 | 0.57 | 0.29 | 0.43 | -- |
| Field Sparrow | 0.14 | 0.14 | 0.14 | 0.29 | 0.43 | 0.14 | 0.33 |
| Gray Catbird | -- | 0.14 | -- | 0.86 | 0.57 | 0.29 | 0.17 |
| Great Crested Flycatcher | -- | -- | -- | 0.29 | 0.14 | -- | -- |
| House Wren | 0.14 | -- | 0.14 | 0.14 | 0.29 | 0.57 | -- |
| **Indigo Bunting** | **0.14** | -- | **0.71** | **0.43** | **0.57** | **0.57** | -- |
| Least Flycatcher* | -- | -- | -- | -- | 0.14 | -- | -- |
| Mourning Dove | -- | 0.43 | -- | 0.14 | 0.43 | 0.43 | 0.17 |
| Northern (Baltimore) Oriole | -- | -- | 0.14 | 0.29 | 0.14 | 0.43 | -- |
| Northern (Yellow-shafted) Flicker | -- | -- | 0.14 | -- | -- | 0.14 | -- |
| Northern Cardinal | 0.29 | 0.43 | 0.71 | 0.86 | 0.57 | 1.29 | 0.33 |
| Northern Mockingbird | -- | -- | -- | -- | -- | 0.14 | -- |
| Orchard Oriole | -- | -- | -- | -- | 0.14 | 0.43 | -- |
| Purple Martin | -- | -- | -- | -- | 0.14 | -- | -- |

Table 5. Number of individuals encountered per plot visit (including flyovers) in woodlands, averaged over plots sampled (n), for bird species recorded at Hopewell Culture National Historical Park, Ohio during breeding bird surveys. Individual species results are listed by year, 2005-2011 (continued).

| Common name | 2005 (n=7) | 2006 (n=7) | 2007 (n=7) | 2008 (n=7) | 2009 (n=7) | 2010 (n=7) | 2011 (n=6) |
|---|---|---|---|---|---|---|---|
| **Red-bellied Woodpecker** | -- | -- | **0.14** | -- | **0.14** | **0.43** | **0.17** |
| Red-eyed Vireo | -- | 0.14 | 0.14 | 0.14 | -- | 0.14 | -- |
| Red-winged Blackbird | 0.29 | 1.23 | 0.14 | 1.29 | 0.43 | 0.71 | 0.33 |
| Ring-necked Pheasant | -- | -- | -- | -- | 0.14 | -- | -- |
| Rock Dove | -- | -- | -- | -- | -- | 0.86 | -- |
| Ruby-throated Hummingbird | -- | -- | -- | 0.14 | -- | -- | -- |
| Scarlet Tanager | -- | -- | -- | 0.14 | -- | -- | -- |
| Song Sparrow | 0.14 | -- | 0.14 | 0.57 | 0.43 | 0.71 | 0.17 |
| Tree Swallow | 0.43 | 0.14 | -- | 0.14 | 0.14 | 0.14 | 0.67 |
| (Eastern) Tufted Titmouse | 0.43 | 0.14 | -- | 0.14 | 0.14 | 0.29 | -- |
| Warbling Vireo | -- | -- | -- | -- | 0.43 | 0.29 | -- |
| White-breasted Nuthatch* | -- | -- | -- | -- | 0.14 | 0.29 | -- |
| **White-eyed Vireo** | -- | -- | -- | **0.43** | **0.14** | -- | -- |
| **Willow Flycatcher** | -- | -- | **0.29** | -- | -- | -- | -- |
| **Wood Thrush** | **0.29** | **0.43** | **0.29** | **0.57** | **0.43** | **0.29** | **0.17** |
| Yellow Warbler | 0.29 | 0.29 | -- | 0.57 | 0.14 | 0.14 | -- |
| Yellow-billed Cuckoo | -- | 0.14 | 0.14 | -- | 0.14 | -- | -- |
| Yellow-breasted Chat | 0.29 | 0.14 | 0.29 | -- | 0.57 | 0.14 | 0.17 |
| **Yellow-throated Vireo** | -- | -- | -- | **0.14** | -- | **0.14** | **0.33** |
| **Yellow-throated Warbler*** | -- | -- | -- | -- | -- | 0.14 | -- |

* Species recorded exclusively in woodland habitats.

Bolded species names are those species considered of continental importance (Rich et al. 2004).

Table 6. Proportion of plots (n) occupied annually by bird species (including flyovers) in woodlands at Hopewell Culture National Historical Park, Ohio during breeding bird surveys. Individual species results are listed by year, 2005-2011.

| Common name | 2005 (n=7) | 2006 (n=7) | 2007 (n=7) | 2008 (n=7) | 2009 (n= 7) | 2010 (n=7) | 2011 (n=6) |
|---|---|---|---|---|---|---|---|
| **Acadian Flycatcher** | -- | -- | **0.14** | -- | -- | **0.14** | -- |
| American Crow | -- | -- | -- | -- | 0.29 | 0.14 | -- |
| American Goldfinch | -- | -- | -- | 0.14 | 0.14 | 0.29 | -- |
| American Redstart* | -- | -- | -- | 0.14 | -- | 0.14 | -- |
| American Robin | 0.43 | 0.57 | 0.57 | 0.14 | 0.86 | 0.71 | 0.43 |
| Belted Kingfisher* | 0.14 | 0.14 | -- | -- | -- | -- | -- |
| Bewick's Wren | -- | 0.43 | -- | -- | -- | -- | -- |
| Blue Jay | -- | -- | 0.14 | 0.43 | 0.14 | 0.29 | 0.29 |
| Blue-gray Gnatcatcher | 0.14 | -- | 0.14 | 0.29 | -- | 0.43 | -- |
| **Blue-winged Warbler** | -- | **0.14** | -- | -- | -- | -- | -- |
| **Brown Thrasher** | -- | -- | -- | **0.14** | **0.14** | -- | **0.14** |
| Brown-headed Cowbird | -- | -- | -- | 0.29 | 0.43 | 0.43 | -- |
| Canada Goose | -- | 0.14 | -- | 0.14 | 0.14 | 0.14 | -- |
| Carolina Chickadee | -- | -- | 0.29 | -- | -- | 0.14 | -- |
| **Carolina Wren** | **0.57** | -- | **0.29** | **0.29** | **0.43** | **0.43** | -- |
| Cedar Waxwing | -- | -- | -- | 0.29 | 0.14 | -- | -- |
| Chipping Sparrow* | -- | -- | -- | -- | 0.14 | 0.14 | 0.14 |
| Chimney Swift | -- | -- | -- | -- | 0.14 | 0.14 | -- |
| Common Grackle | -- | -- | -- | 0.14 | 0.43 | 0.43 | -- |
| Cooper's Hawk | -- | -- | -- | -- | -- | -- | 0.14 |
| Common Yellowthroat | 0.14 | 0.29 | 0.14 | 0.57 | 0.43 | 0.71 | 0.14 |
| Downy Woodpecker | -- | -- | -- | 0.14 | 0.43 | 0.43 | -- |
| **Eastern (Rufous-side) Towhee** | **0.14** | **0.14** | **0.29** | **0.43** | **0.29** | **0.43** | **0.14** |
| Eastern Bluebird | -- | -- | -- | 0.29 | -- | -- | -- |
| Eastern Kingbird | -- | -- | -- | -- | 0.14 | -- | -- |
| Eastern Meadowlark | -- | -- | -- | 0.14 | -- | 0.14 | -- |
| Eastern Wood-pewee | 0.14 | 0.57 | 0.29 | 0.29 | 0.14 | 0.14 | -- |
| European Starling | -- | 0.14 | 0.29 | 0.29 | 0.29 | 0.43 | -- |
| Field Sparrow | 0.14 | 0.14 | 0.14 | 0.29 | 0.43 | 0.14 | 0.29 |
| Gray Catbird | -- | 0.14 | -- | 0.43 | 0.43 | 0.14 | 0.14 |
| Great Crested Flycatcher | -- | -- | -- | 0.14 | 0.14 | -- | -- |
| House Wren | 0.14 | -- | 0.14 | 0.14 | 0.29 | 0.43 | -- |
| **Indigo Bunting** | **0.14** | -- | **0.57** | **0.43** | **0.57** | **0.57** | -- |
| Least Flycatcher* | -- | -- | -- | -- | 0.14 | -- | -- |
| Mourning Dove | -- | 0.29 | -- | 0.14 | 0.43 | 0.14 | 0.14 |
| Northern (Baltimore) Oriole | -- | -- | 0.14 | 0.29 | 0.14 | 0.43 | -- |
| Northern (Yellow-shafted) Flicker | -- | -- | 0.14 | -- | -- | 0.14 | -- |
| Northern Cardinal | 0.29 | 0.43 | 0.57 | 0.71 | 0.57 | 1.00 | 0.29 |
| Northern Mockingbird | -- | -- | -- | -- | -- | 0.14 | -- |
| Orchard Oriole | -- | -- | -- | -- | 0.14 | 0.14 | -- |
| Purple Martin | -- | -- | -- | -- | 0.14 | -- | -- |

Table 6. Proportion of plots (n) occupied annually by bird species (including flyovers) in woodlands at Hopewell Culture National Historical Park, Ohio during breeding bird surveys. Individual species results are listed by year, 2005-2011 (continued).

| Common name | 2005 (n=7) | 2006 (n=7) | 2007 (n=7) | 2008 (n=7) | 2009 (n=7) | 2010 (n=7) | 2011 (n=6) |
|---|---|---|---|---|---|---|---|
| **Red-bellied Woodpecker** | -- | -- | 0.14 | -- | 0.14 | 0.43 | 0.14 |
| Red-eyed Vireo | -- | 0.14 | 0.14 | 0.14 | -- | 0.14 | -- |
| Red-winged Blackbird | 0.29 | 0.29 | 0.14 | 0.43 | 0.43 | 0.43 | 0.29 |
| Ring-necked Pheasant | -- | -- | -- | -- | 0.14 | -- | -- |
| Rock Dove | -- | -- | -- | -- | -- | 0.14 | -- |
| Ruby-throated Hummingbird | -- | -- | -- | 0.14 | -- | -- | -- |
| Scarlet Tanager | -- | -- | -- | 0.14 | -- | -- | -- |
| Song Sparrow | 0.14 | -- | 0.14 | 0.57 | 0.43 | 0.57 | 0.14 |
| Tree Swallow | 0.14 | 0.14 | -- | 0.14 | 0.14 | 0.14 | 0.14 |
| (Eastern) Tufted Titmouse | 0.29 | 0.14 | -- | 0.14 | 0.14 | 0.29 | -- |
| Warbling Vireo | -- | -- | -- | -- | 0.14 | 0.29 | -- |
| White-breasted Nuthatch* | -- | -- | -- | -- | 0.14 | 0.14 | -- |
| **White-eyed Vireo** | -- | -- | -- | 0.43 | 0.14 | -- | -- |
| **Willow Flycatcher** | -- | -- | 0.29 | -- | -- | -- | -- |
| **Wood Thrush** | 0.29 | 0.43 | 0.29 | 0.57 | 0.43 | 0.29 | 0.14 |
| Yellow Warbler | 0.29 | 0.14 | -- | 0.43 | 0.14 | 0.14 | -- |
| Yellow-billed Cuckoo | -- | 0.14 | 0.14 | -- | 0.14 | -- | -- |
| Yellow-breasted Chat | 0.29 | 0.14 | 0.14 | -- | 0.29 | 0.14 | 0.14 |
| **Yellow-throated Vireo** | -- | -- | -- | 0.14 | -- | 0.14 | 0.29 |
| **Yellow-throated Warbler*** | -- | -- | -- | -- | -- | 0.14 | -- |

\* Species recorded exclusively in woodland habitats.

Bolded species names are those species considered of continental importance (Rich et al. 2004).

## Bird Habitat

Bird survey plots on HOCU are located primarily in grassland and old field habitat types, with a lesser amount of woodland habitat present (Fig. 2). On grassland (open) plots cool season grass, forbs, total foliar cover, and structural diversity index value were similar across years (Fig. 3). Grass litter was also similar across years (Fig. 4). However, bare soil declined in 2007 and remained lower in 2011. Total unvegetated area on grassland (open) plots declined in 2011.

Hardwood basal area, canopy cover, and canopy height, varied slightly across years on woodland plots (Fig. 5). On woodland plots cool season grass and structural diversity index value were similar across years (Fig. 6). However, forbs, shrubs and vines, and total foliar cover demonstrated some variability between years. Bare soil, deciduous litter, and woody debris were variable between years (Fig. 7). However, total unvegetated area on woodland plots remained similar across years. Trees from the *Aceraceae* and *Rosaceae* families dominated the hardwood species annually, thus canopy cover, canopy height, and basal area (Fig. 8).

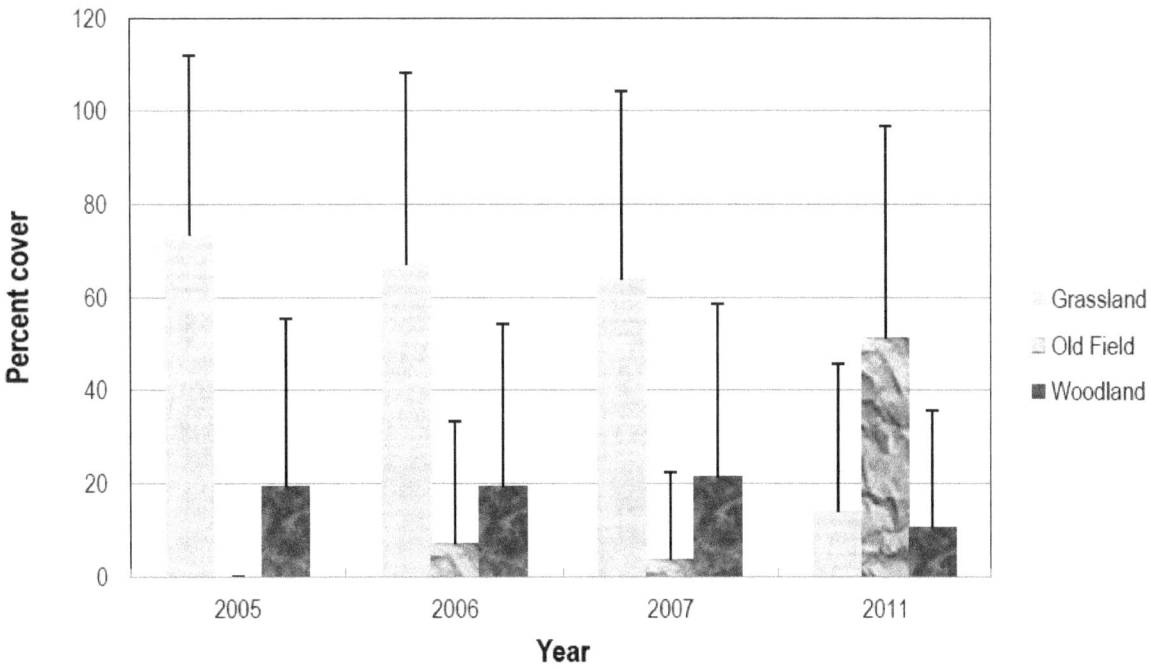

Figure 2. Average (±std dev) coverage of habitats recorded on 50-m plots at Hopewell Culture National Historical Park, Ohio during breeding bird monitoring in 2005, 2006, 2007, and 2011.

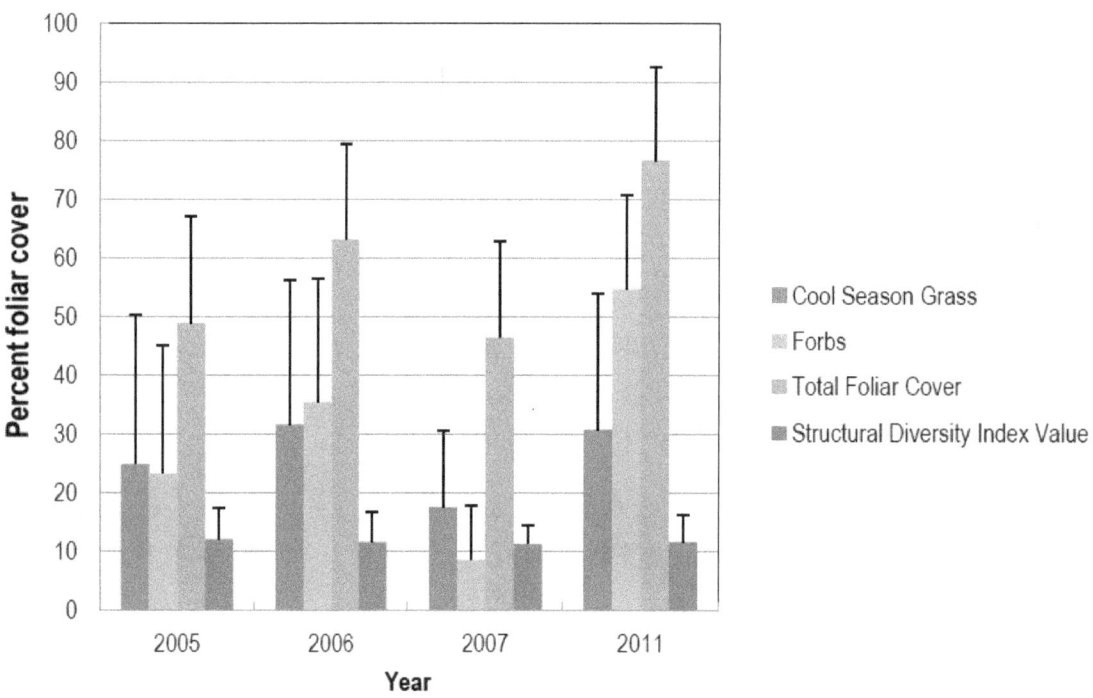

Figure 3. Average (±std dev) foliar cover and vegetation structural diversity recorded on grassland (open) plots at Hopewell Culture National Historical Park, Ohio during breeding bird monitoring in 2005, 2006, 2007, and 2011.

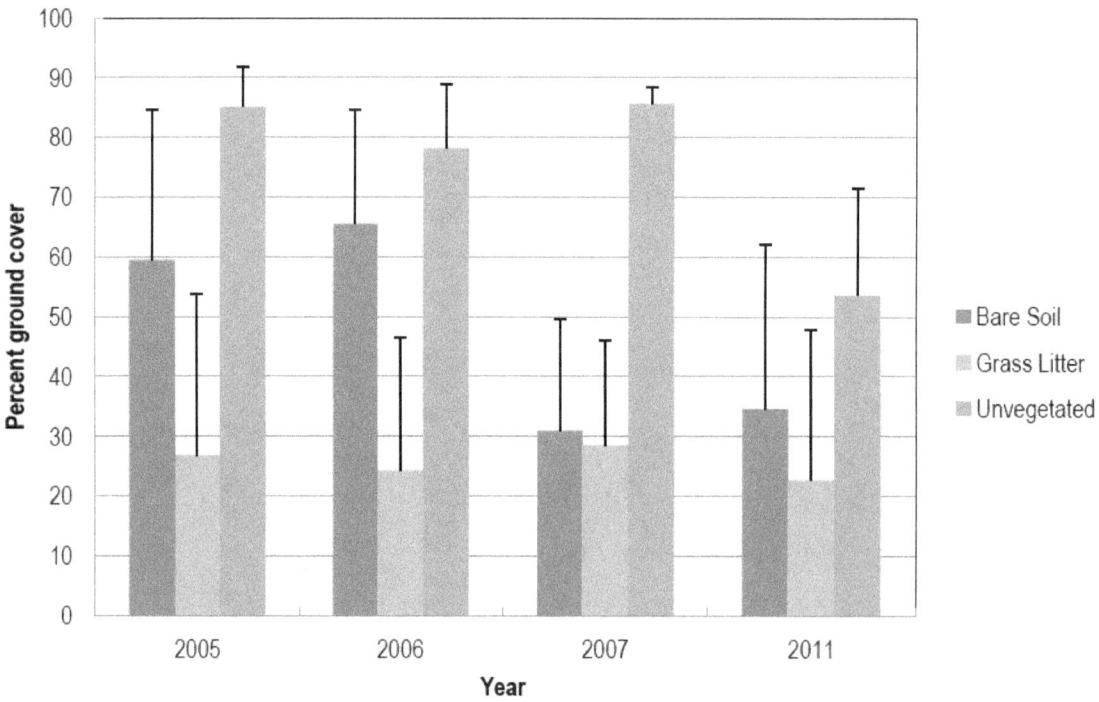

Figure 4. Average (±std dev) ground cover recorded on grassland (open) plots at Hopewell Culture National Historical Park, Ohio during breeding bird monitoring in 2005, 2006, 2007, and 2011.

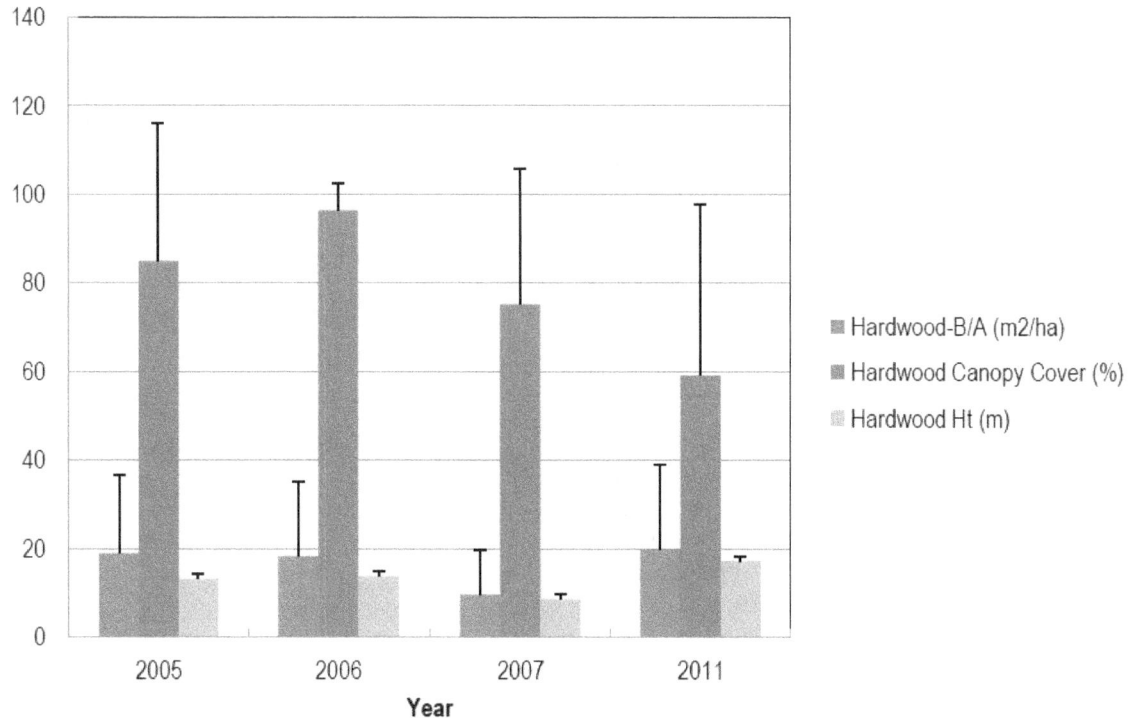

Figure 5. Average (±std dev) hardwood basal area, canopy cover, and tree height recorded on woodland plots at Hopewell Culture National Historical Park, Ohio during breeding bird monitoring in 2005, 2006, 2007, and 2011.

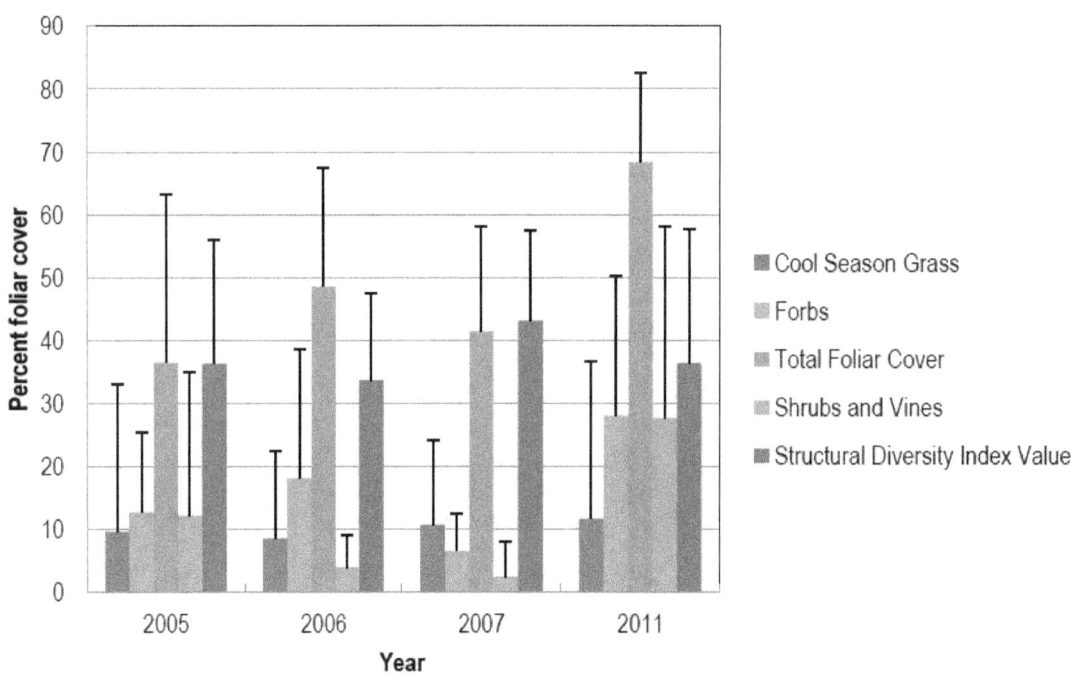

Figure 6. Average (±std dev) foliar cover and vegetation structural diversity recorded on woodland plots at Hopewell Culture National Historical Park, Ohio during breeding bird monitoring in 2005, 2006, 2007, and 2011.

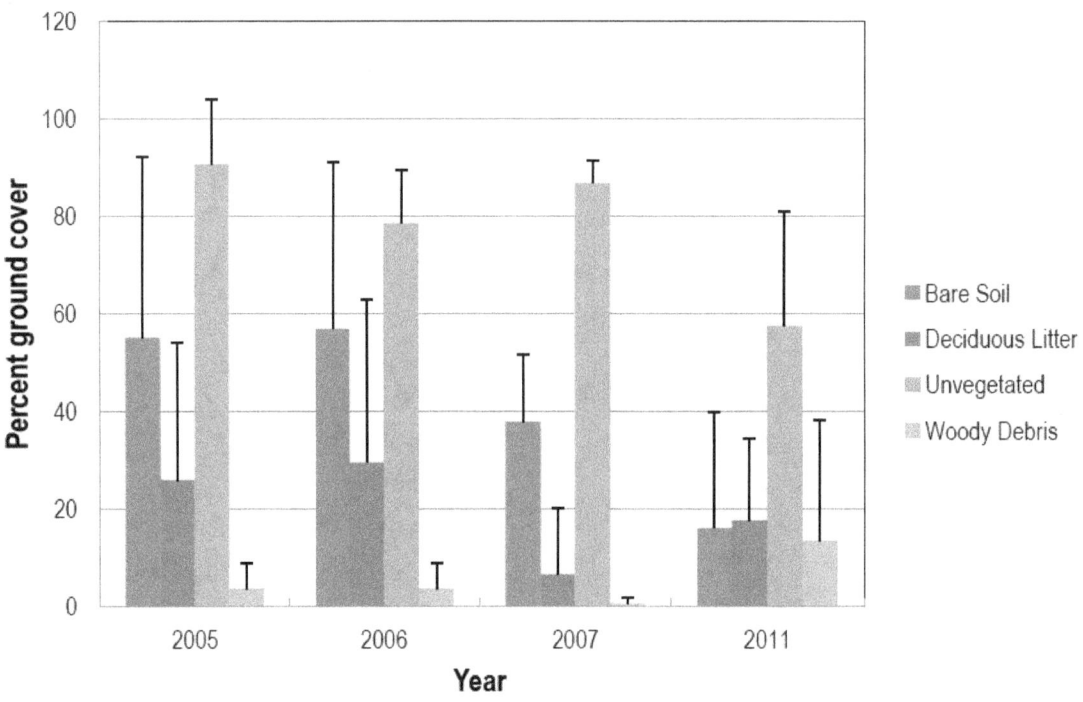

Figure 7. Average (±std dev) ground cover recorded on woodland plots at Hopewell Culture National Historical Park, Ohio during breeding bird monitoring in 2005, 2006, 2007, and 2011.

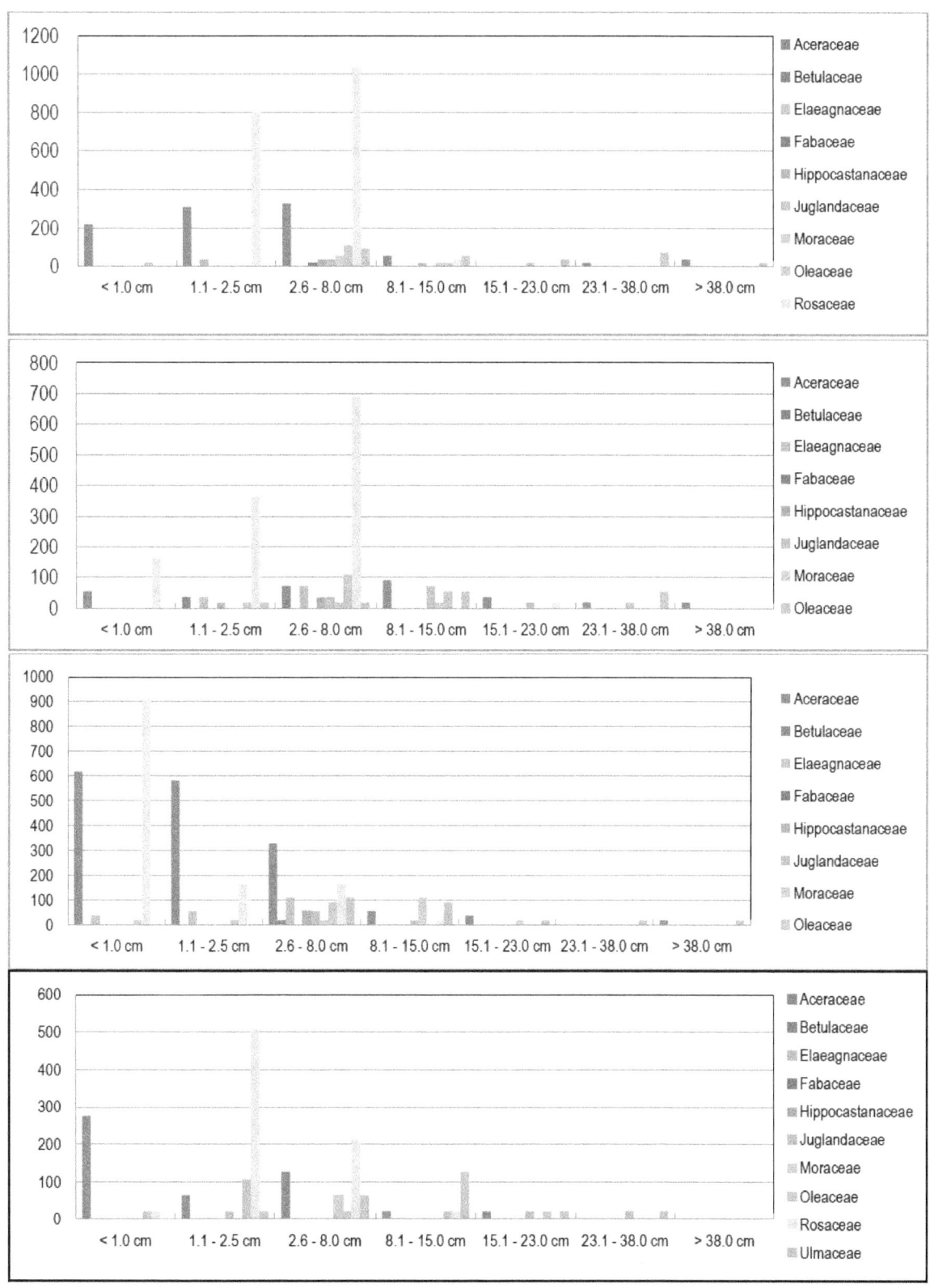

Figure 8. Stems per hectare by size class for tree families recorded on Hopewell Culture National Historical Park, Ohio during breeding bird monitoring in 2005, 2006, 2007, and 2011 (top to bottom).

# Summary

Bird surveys and habitat assessment work were initiated at HOCU in 2005, to assist the park in assessing the ecological integrity of habitat on the park through time. Eighty-nine of the 96 bird species recorded are permanent or summer residents to the area (Stokes and Stokes 1995). Therefore, these species have some value in characterizing the breeding bird community of HOCU through time.

Grassland (open) habitats and a lesser component of woodlands dominate HOCU. This mix of habitats across the park is a contributing factor to the rich and diverse bird community observed. But, the rich mix and positioning of these habitats on the park units makes it difficult to elucidate relationships between bird richness and habitats. However, the current efforts to restore native grassland habitat on HOCU, will favor the 20 breeding species observed exclusively in grassland (open) habitats, especially the six grassland obligates species. Changes in habitat from grasslands to old fields between 2007 and 2011, illustrates the parks efforts to convert non-native grassland to native grasslands. The first step in restoring native grasses to non-native grasslands is to covert the grasslands to old field by eradicating the non-native grasses. Although, management of the woodland habitat on HOCU is a lower priority then grassland (open) habitat, the seven species recorded exclusively in this habitat would benefit from any actions aimed at improving or expanding this habitat type. Present habitats on HOCU meet the varied requirements of the 15 breeding species of continental importance observed. However, shifts in the composition of species of continental importance may occur as grassland habitats become more prominent.

# Literature Cited

Cairns Jr., J., P.V. McCormick and B.R. Niederlehner. 2004. A proposed framework for developing indicators of ecosystem health. Hydrobiologia 263:1-44.

Fancy, S. G. 1997. A new approach for analyzing bird densities from variable circular-plot counts. Pacific Science 51:107-114.

ITIS (Integrated Taxonomic Information System). http://www.itis.usda.gov/.

Johnson, D.H., L.D. Igl, J.A. Dechant, M.L. Sondreal, C.M. Goldade, M.P. Nenneman, and B.R. Euliss. 1998. Effects of management practices on grassland birds. Northern Prairie Wildlife Research Center, Jamestown, North Dakota. http://www.npwrc.usgs.gov/resource/literatr/grasbird/index.htm

Karr, J.R. 1991. Biological integrity: a long-neglected aspect of water resource management. Ecological Applications 1:66-84.

Karr, J.R. and D.R. Dudley. 1981. Ecological perspective on water quality goals. Environmental Management 5:55-68.

Mallory, M.L., H.G. Gilchrist, B.M. Braune and A.J. Gaston. 2006. Marine birds as indicators of arctic marine ecosystem health: linking the northern ecosystem initiative to long-term studies. Environmental Monitoring and Assessment 113:31-48.

Maurer, B.A. 1993. Biological diversity, ecological integrity, and neotropical migrants: New perspectives for wildlife managers. Pages 24-31 in D.M. Finch and P.W. Stangel, editors. Status and management of neotropical migratory birds. U.S. Forest Service General Technical Report RM-229.

Peitz, D.G., G.A. Rowell, J.L. Haack, K.M. James, L.W. Morrison, and M.D. DeBacker. 2008. Breeding bird monitoring protocol for the Heartland Network Inventory and Monitoring Program. Natural Resource Report NPS/HTLN/NRR-2008/044. National Park Service, Fort Collins, Colorado. 152pp.

Rich, T.D., C.J. Beardmore, H. Berlanga, P.J. Blancher, M.S.W. Bradstreet, G.S. Butcher, D.W. Demarest, E.H. Dunn, W.C. Hunter, E.E. Inigo-Elias, J.A. Kennedy, A.M. Martell. A.O. Panjabi, D.N. Pashley, K.V. Rosenberg, C.M. Rustay, J.S. Wendt, T.C. Will. 2004. Partners in Flight North American Landbird Conservation Plan. Cornell Lab of Ornithology, Ithaca, New York. 84pp.

Stokes, D.W. and L.Q. Stokes. 1995. Stokes Field Guide to Birds: Eastern Region. Little, Brown and Company, New York, New York. 471 pp.

Winter, M. 1998. Effect of habitat fragmentation on grassland-nesting birds in southwestern Missouri. Ph.D. dissertation, University of Missouri, Columbia.

Wood, J.K., N. Nur, C.A. Howell and G.R. Geupel. 2006. Overview of Cosumnes riparian bird study and recommendations for monitoring and management. A Report to the California Bay-Delta Authority Ecosystem Restoration Program. Petaluma, California.

www.ingramcontent.com/pod-product-compliance
Lightning Source LLC
Chambersburg PA
CBHW080938290526
45795CB00007BA/2803